Cause, Effect, Chaos!

Animal Kingdom

Author Paul Mason
with artwork by Mark Ruffle

Enslow PUBLISHING

The website addresses (URLs) included in this book were valid at the time of going to press. However, it is possible that contents or addresses may have changed since the publication of this book. No responsibility for any such change can be accepted by either the author or the Publisher.

Published in 2026 by Enslow Publishing, LLC
2544 Clinton Street
Buffalo, NY 14224

First published in Great Britain in 2018 by Wayland

Series editor: Paul Rockett
Series design and illustration: Mark Ruffle
www.rufflebrothers.com

Manufactured in the United States of America

CPSIA compliance information: Batch #CSENS26: For further information contact Enslow Publishing LLC, New York, New York at 1-800-398-2504.

Please visit our website, www.enslowpublishing.com. For a free color catalog of all our high-quality books, call toll free 1-800-398-2504 or fax 1-877-980-4454.

Cataloging-in-Publication Data
Names: Mason, Paul. | Ruffle, Mark, illustrator.
Title: Animal kingdom / Paul Mason ; illustrated by Mark Ruffle.
Description: Buffalo, NY : Enslow Publishing, 2026. |
Series: Cause, effect, chaos! | Includes glossary and index.
Identifiers: ISBN 9781978545205 (pbk.) | ISBN 9781978545212 (library bound) |
ISBN 9781978545229 (ebook)
Subjects: LCSH: Animals--Juvenile literature.
Classification: LCC QL40.M376 2026 | DDC 590--dc23

Contents

Cause and Effect

"Cause and effect" is a way of describing how one event leads to another. Often, the second event leads to a third and so on, creating a whole string of events.

You will be able to think of examples from your own life ...

Cause:
You stay at your friend's house for one extra round of the new dance game.

Effect 1:
Because you are a bit late leaving, you get caught in a rain shower.

Your new sneakers are wrecked.

Of course, the chain of cause and effect may not end there:

Effect 2:
The extra dance practice pays off when you score a big role in your school's next show.

In the animal kingdom, cause and effect is sometimes a matter of life and death.

Brown snowshoe hares start growing a new coat around October 10. The coat is white: camouflage for the snowy winter.

When the snow begins to melt on about April 10, the hares start to grow a brown coat again. It is their summer camouflage.

Unfortunately, though,

the hares' timing is not always perfect.

Some years, the snow comes late or spring comes early.
The hares change color out of time with their surroundings.

This can cause **chaos** and put the hares' lives in danger.

They stand out against the wrong-colored background for every predator to see.

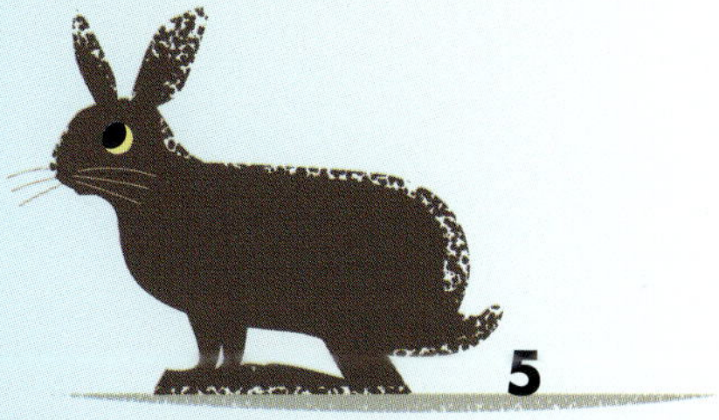

The Crazy-ant Menace!

Every year at the same time on Christmas Island in the Indian Ocean, the ground is carpeted in red crabs.

Millions of Christmas Island red crabs leave their burrows in the forest floor. They are heading for the sea to breed. Their journey is a perilous one.

The wet season signals the crabs to emerge from their underground homes.

The first danger they face is sunshine.

Crabs must stay moist to survive: if the sun appears, they dry out.

Some crabs hide from the sun under rocks or plants.

As the red crabs head for the sea, giant robber crabs pounce and eat some.

Millions escape–but they are not safe yet ...

Around 100 years ago, yellow crazy ants were introduced onto Christmas Island. The population of crazy ants has grown to billions!

The yellow crazy ants spray acid into the crabs' eyes and joints. The crabs become immobile ant food.

Due to the crazy ants, the number of crabs on Christmas Island is falling.

This is causing **chaos** for the island. Without crab burrows, the soil changes. Different plants start to grow, affecting the other animals that live there.

To combat the ant menace, tiny wasps have been introduced. Scientists think the wasps will quickly control ant numbers.

Salmon Spawners

Every summer, millions of salmon leave the sea and head upriver. They are going back to where they spawned, to reproduce before they die.

On Kodiak Island in Alaska, hungry bears lie in wait–or at least, they should.

The salmon enter the river and begin to swim upstream.

Bears gather at the best fishing places.

The biggest bears get the best fishing spots.

The bears eat as much salmon as possible, ready for winter hibernation, when they will live off their body's store of energy.

Uneaten bits of salmon are left in the nearby forests. They rot and add nutrients to the soil.

Summers on Kodiak Island have been getting warmer. This is causing chaos!

Bears love elderberries. They have been eating those instead of salmon.

Red elderberries now ripen earlier, at the same time as the salmon arrive.

Most salmon die after spawning. Instead of being eaten by bears, their bodies just float off downstream.

The soil no longer gets nutrients from salmon carcasses.

It becomes harder for plants to grow, including the elderberries the bears love so much. The forest animals end up with less to eat.

The Quiet Killer

Barn owls hunt mostly in the dark. They are deadly hunters and catch their prey about 75 percent of the time.

Compare this with, for example, lions (where the success rate is 30 percent) or peregrine falcons (47 percent). What is it that makes barn owls such good hunters?

The hunt begins with the owl flying quietly along, listening for prey.

The owl's disc-like face funnels sound to the owl's ear, so it hears if the prey moves. It drops down head first. Even now, the owl's victim may not hear it coming.

When it hears a vole, mouse, or rat, the owl hovers above until it is sure where the prey is.

At the last minute, the owl swings its talons through to grab its victim.

Barn owls do sometimes miss, and they have other problems too, because modern farms are changing.

Farms have fewer old, wooden buildings for owls to roost in.

Poisons that are used to kill rats and other rodents remain in the body of owl prey and can poison owls that eat them.

Today, the number of barn owls has fallen. Some experts think there are less than half as many as 100 years ago.

Tigers that Come for Dinner

In the forests of South Asia, the Bengal tiger is an apex predator. It hunts whatever meat it can kill, but nothing–except humans–hunts tigers.

Tigers hunt mostly deer and wild cattle, but they also kill wild boar, monkeys, and other animals.

The tiger sees or smells prey nearby. It makes sure it is downwind, so the victim will not smell it coming.

The tiger creeps closer.

Its special, flexible shoulders allow it to walk with its belly almost on the ground.

When the tiger is close enough, it races forwards. Tigers can sprint 30 miles (50 km) per hour over short distances.

The tiger aims to bite its prey on the neck, crushing its windpipe. The prey **suffocates.**

Elderly or sick tigers are too slow to catch normal prey such as deer.

They have to find something slower for their dinner–such as local villagers!

In South Asia, about 100 people a year are attacked and killed by tigers.

The Dragon's Bite

There are no actual fire-breathing dragons in the world. The closest thing we have is a giant lizard known as a Komodo dragon, from Indonesia.

The Komodo's breath may not be fiery, but it is foul. And this dragon is dangerous to large animals and humans.

The Komodo dragon lies in wait for its victims. Its brown skin is good camouflage among the plants and rocks.

The dragon flicks out its tongue to sense approaching victims–including people.

Komodos have poor hearing and vision, but a good sense of smell. They use their forked tongue to "taste" the air and find out who's around.

When the prey is close enough, the dragon lunges forwards and seizes it in its jaws.

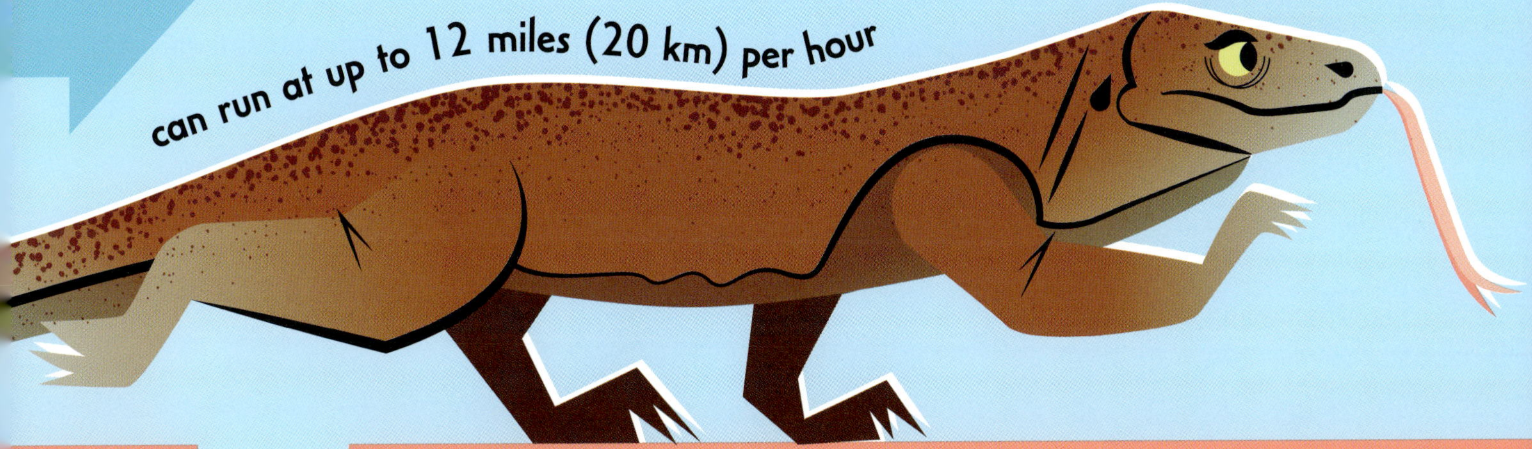

can run at up to 12 miles (20 km) per hour

The smell of blood attracts other dragons ...

which can smell blood and rotting flesh from 5 miles (8 km) away.

If the prey pulls free and escapes, the bite keeps bleeding. It contains **anticoagulants,** and may be poisonous.

Eventually, the poison takes effect and the bitten prey becomes weak and collapses.

When this happens ... the Komodo dragons are waiting.

Polar Peril!

Each spring in the Arctic, polar bears leave their winter hibernation. They head for the sea ice to hunt seals.

The bears need to eat plenty over the coming months to build up energy reserves for their next hibernation.

The bear heads for the hole, then waits patiently for the seal to come up for a breath.

Bears sniff out food.

A bear can smell a seal at a breathing hole a 0.5 mile (1 km) away.

As the seal surfaces, the bear pounces.

More often than not, the seal escapes.

Some bears go looking for food on land. Their white coats are not camouflaged, so hunting is tricky.

There is food around human settlements, but bear-human contact is dangerous for both sides. Many bears have been shot, and a few people have been

killed by bears.

Bears need to make lots of attacks and hunt over a large area. But our planet is getting warmer. **There is less ice in the Arctic**, so the polar bears' hunting ground is shrinking.

The ice melts sooner and forms later each year.

The bears find it harder to store up fat reserves for winter.

The Snake that Stuffs Itself

When baby boa constrictors are born, they are about 15 inches (40 cm) long. They hunt small creatures such as mice. But boa constrictors never stop growing …

By 25 years old, some boa constrictors are nearly 13 feet (4 m) long! A snake that big can hunt almost anything.

The snake hides, flicking out its tongue to taste the air for prey.

As the prey gets closer it causes vibrations in the ground and air, which the snake feels.

When it sees its prey, the snake makes a lightning-fast strike.

A boa constrictor's backward-curving teeth are hard to escape.

The snake wraps itself around its victim's body and squeezes. A lack of oxygen soon causes the prey to die.

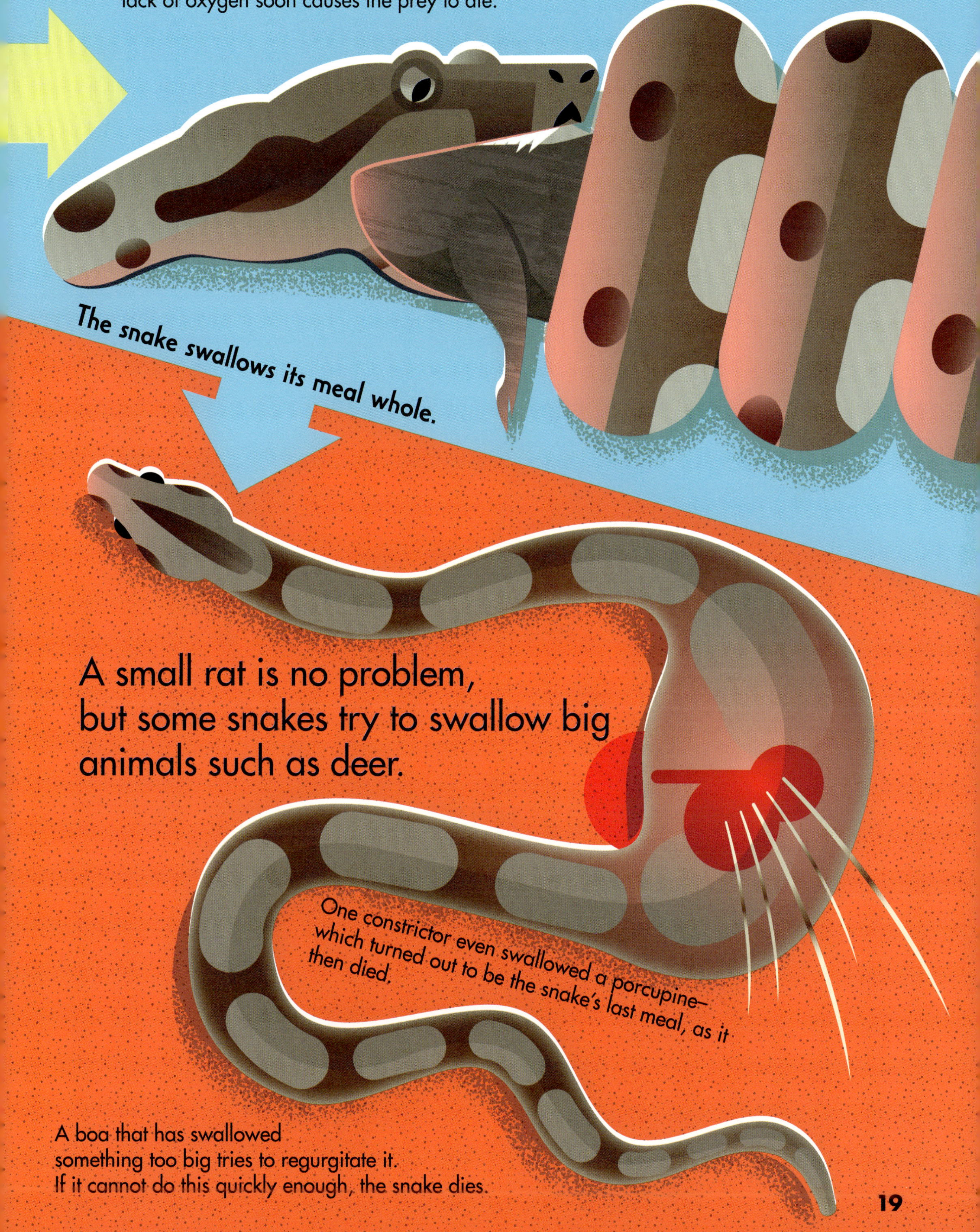

The snake swallows its meal whole.

A small rat is no problem, but some snakes try to swallow big animals such as deer.

One constrictor even swallowed a porcupine—which turned out to be the snake's last meal, as it then died.

A boa that has swallowed something too big tries to regurgitate it. If it cannot do this quickly enough, the snake dies.

Watch Out! Crocodiles About

Every year, wildebeest migrate around the Serengeti plains of Africa in search of fresh grazing.

On their journey, the wildebeest face all kinds of dangers–plus some particularly chaotic river crossings.

In January, the herds head south. Between now and March, their calves will be born.

The survivors make it back to the northern feeding grounds by **August.** They stay until rains further south cause new grass to grow in **November.**

Because calves are an easy meal, predators follow the herds to the southern Serengeti.

By April and May, the southern grasses are running out. The herds move towards fresh pastures in the central and western Serengeti.

The most dangerous part of their journey is next.

In July, the wildebeest reach the wide, murky rivers of the western Serengeti. Waiting in the waters are hungry Nile crocodiles.

The crossing is chaos!

Even if they make it across, a few wildebeest are dragged back in by the crocodiles.

Although many wildebeest die during the migration, far more would starve if they did not travel to find fresh food.

Moth Love Potion

Like many insects, a moth's life cycle is fascinating. Moths don't start life as moths at all. They go through three other shapes first.

A moth's life is also hazardous. In fact, dangers lurk at every step of the way.

Moths start life as eggs, usually laid on leaves.

Insects and small birds eat the eggs.

Cunning wasps even inject their own eggs into the moth eggs, giving newly hatched wasp grubs something to eat.

The surviving eggs hatch into caterpillars. Birds, mice, and some insects all eat moth caterpillars.

Any caterpillar that survives becomes a pupa. Pupae are eaten by birds, spiders, frogs, toads, and snakes.

Finally, a young moth emerges from the pupa. It spreads its wings, ready to fly.

The female moth gives off a love potion scent. But sadly, half of all moths are eaten before they can find a mate!

The spider throws out a sticky gob of thread and lassos the moth to capture and eat it. With that, another moth is gone.

If a male moth does smell a female, it heads in her direction. But the chaos isn't over. Sometimes, the moth love scent is released by a sneaky bolas spider. **Uh-oh ...**

Only one moth egg in 400 manages to become a breeding adult and start the cycle again.

The Tentacled* Terror!

Multi-armed sea monsters that attack sailors don't actually exist–but the giant Pacific octopus does.

This octopus is said to reach an arm span of over 26 feet (8 m), and weigh three times as much as a grown man. It is also a deadly hunter.

It bites down with its sharp beak.

Sometimes octopuses inject venom into their prey, leaving it unable to move.

At night, the octopus leaves its den and feels its way along the sea floor. Octopus arms have taste buds, so it tastes whatever it touches.

When it touches prey the octopus grabs it, holding on with suckers on its arms.

*We shouldn't really call them tentacles: the proper name is "arms."

The octopus heads for a den or safe place to eat.

If a predator such as a shark appears, the octopus changes color to camouflage itself, or squirts out a cloud of ink.

Sometimes octopuses wave one arm around for predators to bite off. The arm carries on wriggling, the octopus escapes, and the arm grows back later.

Overfishing, especially of sharks, means there are fewer predators around, and more octopuses.

The tentacled terrors are **taking over** the oceans, and who knows, maybe they'll crawl onto the land next ... *

*Don't worry! All octopuses need water to breathe, so they can only stay on land for a short time.

The Cat with a Sore Paw

Cheetahs are the fastest predators on land. In 2012, a cheetah called Sarah was recorded running at almost 62 miles (100 km) per hour.

Cheetahs are built for speed, not endurance. They need to catch their prey quickly—and that's not the only challenge they face.

The black stripes beside a cheetah's eyes may stop it from being dazzled by the sun.

When a cheetah sees prey, it begins to move slowly towards it.

The cheetah aims to get within 100 feet (30 m) before being spotted.

When the prey runs, the cheetah sprints after it.

Its claws act like spiked running shoes, giving extra grip.

At top speed, the cheetah takes more than three strides per second.

When it is close enough, the cheetah swipes the prey to the ground.

It bites the prey's neck to kill it.

Cheetahs are successful about half the time– but even when they catch prey, chaos can still occur ...

Animals such as lions and hyenas steal about half of what cheetahs catch.

A cheetah that damages a muscle or treads on a thorn cannot hunt for days.

Without food, a cheetah lacks energy for hunting. If it has cubs, they go hungry and may even die.

The Lonely Rhinos

The world is a tough place for wild animals. They are hunted and affected by habitat loss. Some animals have become extinct as a result.

One animal teetering on the brink of extinction is the northern white rhino.

Years ago, thousands of northern white rhinos roamed across central Africa.

Then they began to be hunted as trophies. By 1960 there were only 2,000 left.

During the 1980s, demand increased for rhino horn to use in Chinese and Vietnamese medicine. Rhino horn does not actually have any medicinal value.

Even so, a small pile of ground-down horn became more valuable than gold or diamonds.

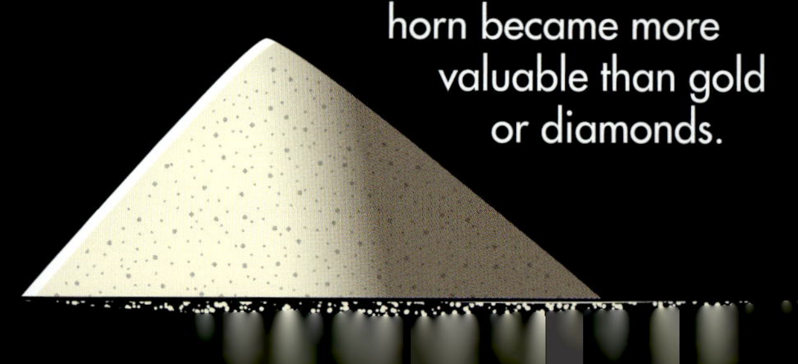

Poachers began killing rhinos to saw off their horns for sale.

Poachers have even killed rhinos living in zoos.

Rhino numbers fell dramatically, and by 2010 no northern white rhinos were left in the wild.

In 2018, the last male northern white rhino died. As of 2024, only two females are left.

Every extinct species is a **disaster** for the world. Species diversity, whether in rhinos, plants, or sharks, ensures a balanced ecosystem where each lifeform has a role to play. The removal of one species impacts the life of all surrounding creatures.

Glossary

anticoagulant chemical that makes blood thinner, and stops it from forming clots or a scab that seals a cut

apex predator predator at the top of the food chain, which no other animal hunts

breathing hole hole in ice where seals and other animals come to the surface to breathe

burrow underground tunnel in which an animal lives

calf the name for a young cow, wildebeest, buffalo, elephant, whale, etc.

camouflage colored disguise that blends into the background

carcass dead body

den hiding place or shelter of a wild animal, such as a fox, bear, mink, or stoat

downwind in the direction the wind is blowing

endurance ability to do something, such as run, for a long time

extinct die out completely, when one type of animal or plant can no longer be found living on Earth

graze eat grass or other plants

habitat natural home of an animal

habitat loss destruction of a habitat (this usually means destruction that has happened because of human activity)

hibernation time during winter when an animal goes into a deep sleep, slowing its breathing and reducing its body temperature

immobile not able to move

joint connection between two bones, which allows movement. Examples are elbows and knees.

nutrient something that living creatures can use for life and growth

overfishing catching of so many fish that they cannot reproduce quickly enough to replace the ones that have been caught

poacher someone who illegally catches and kills animals

predator an animal that kills and feeds on other animals

regurgitate bring food that has been swallowed back up into the mouth

roost place where birds rest at night

spawn release eggs

suffocate deprive of air, so that the victim dies

venom poisonous substance produced by some animals, such as snakes and spiders

Finding Out More

Books

Hughes, Sloane. *20 Things You Didn't Know About Amphibian Adaptations.* Buffalo, NY: PowerKids Press, 2023.

Hughes, Sloane. *20 Things You Didn't Know About Sea Animal Adaptations.* Buffalo, NY: PowerKids Press, 2023.

Filipek, Nina. *Animals.* Buffalo, NY: Gareth Stevens Publishing, 2025.

Websites

Animals
https://kids.nationalgeographic.com/animals
Discover more about animals here.

Lincoln Children's Zoo
https://www.lincolnzoo.org/animals/
Read up on animals found in this zoo.

Index